ELIZABETH MERCURIO

DOLL

LILY POETRY REVIEW BOOKS

Copyright © 2019 by

Published by Lily Poetry Review Books
223 Winter Street
Whitman, MA 02382

https://lilypoetryreview.blog/

ISBN: 978-1-7337683-6-8

All rights reserved. Published in the United States by Lily Poetry Review Books.
Library of Congress Control Number: 2019954728

Cover Design: Martha McCollough
Cover Art: *Broken Doll* by Nathalie Boisard-Beudin

ACKNOWLEDGEMENTS

Grateful acknowledgment is due to the following publications where these poems (or versions of them) have appeared.
Third Point Press, "Doll"
Philadelphia Stories, "Nights of Angels"
The Literary Nest, "Jasmine Fence"
The Skinny Poetry Journal, "Stay" and "Nights,"
Fledgling Rag Issue 18, "The Great Dishonesty of the Precipice, Its Edge"
Lily Poetry Review, "Inward" and "Camille Claudel at the Museum in Paris"

GRATITUDE

I would like to thank the following poets/writers who have inspired and encouraged me:

My Solstice Family: Especially, Laure-Anne Bosselaar, Dzvinia Orlowsky, Kathi Aguero, Nicole Terez Dutton, Iain Haley Pollock, Lisa Sullivan, Colleen DeCourcy, Anderson Evans, Eileen Cleary, Quintin Collins, Konner Jebb, Daniel Summerhill, Meg Kearney, and Beth Little.

Pennsylvania poets/writers: Le Hinton, Jeff Rath, Christine Lincoln, Greg Bachman, Kara Valore, Keith Baughman, and Michele Baughman.

A special thank you to Eileen Cleary and Lily Poetry Review Books for believing in my work and assembling this beautiful chapbook.

I also wish to thank my husband Dante, my children, and my family and friends for their love and support.

Table of Contents

1 INWARD
2 ASLANT A BROOK
4 CAMILLE CLAUDEL AT THE MUSEUM IN PARIS
5 THE VIOLETS
6 NIGHTS OF ANGELS
7 NIGHTS,
8 DOLL
9 STAY
10 ANOTHER MORNING AT THE STARLIGHT HOTEL
11 THE ROSES
12 MORE ANGEL THAN BIRD
13 JASMINE FENCE
14 SUICIDE, SEXY BONES, AND SHOES THAT JUST MIGHT FIT
15 THE CONSOLATION OF FLOWERS
16 THE GREAT DISHONESTY OF THE PRECIPICE, ITS EDGE

Inward

I wake on the tile floor—face flushed.

Gardenias.   I smell gardenias,

    like the kind my favorite teacher brings to school

    and floats in clear bowls.

Angry, the nurse helps me back to bed.
*If I can't trust you,
I'll tie on the restraints.*

    I can't explain why I failed, how I managed
    to push those pills past the tongue's fight.
    I need to keep my legs from shaking
    on this green gurney.

    Ringing ears, different voices,
    the same question—
    why would a pretty girl like you do this?

I stay silent

    rub my fingers over the thin gown

    just between my ribs—

    where an orange-red terror bird twists from my heart.

    I slip inward—
        no longer afraid,

        almost buried.

Aslant a Brook

GERTRUDE
    I saw the willow snap,
        and the body fall.

    Watched the clothes fill
        in murky shallows,

    saw the billow of skirt.
        Heard her mad song.

    My pleasure will come
        in the telling.

    How they will hang
        on my every word.

    Breathe in —
        rosemary, fennel, and rue

    my feet sink in silt
        as words shape in my mind

    ready to spill to the ground as lies.

OPHELIA
>	Don't pull me, from the river,
>>	this cold.
>
>	Bloodwater forces and fills the lungs,
>>	death by misadventure
>
>	some will say. Better to die
>>	than live, like a pawn
>
>	played out to force another's hand.
>
>	There are many foolish ways
>>	to die.
>
>	Death doesn't care.

Camille Claudel at the Museum in Paris

Her face pale, in a dark dress. Sculptor
        hands, idle in her lap. Sculptor hands,

with no clay to tempt them. The delicate girl her hands made.
        She caressed, and caressed—to make a girl.

Whose face I long to touch. Whose face
        reminds me—

Her mother denied her release.
        The mother who never kissed her.

Thirty years in an asylum.

Camille, whose face I long to touch.
        Her gaze, my own.

The Violets

They twist from snowy soil,

>   —resilient violets. Optimistic heart-
> shaped leaves, five perfect petals, on each fragile stem.

>   Grandmother dug violets
> out of the Kentucky soil
> to carry home to her black-lunged father.

After he died, they sent her to a convent.

>   Each spring she looked for them:

>   common blue   marsh blue   bird's foot   sweet white
> —a sob caught in her throat.

For years, she pressed them in her bible, wore them on her sweater,
>   set her table with them on the fine tablecloth.

>   She sent me a pot of them, wild yellow
> on my sixteenth birthday, the day I wrote:

>>   *Dear Grandmother, please don't worry about me.*
>> *I didn't really want*
>> *to die.*

Nights of Angels

They escape convent walls—
        a blizzard of angels,
                little girls in white nightgowns.
They race across the frost-bit ground,
        filthy feet & fragile wings—
by day, they're put away,
        beneath stained glass windows.
                Small hands,
no mothers to warm them.
        Unholy sisters,
                pass down a catechism
of loveless mothers,
        to daughters.
                At eighteen they escape
into watercolor light,
        the cold pink breath
                of Sunday morning.

Nights,

with teeth,

       She held her breath—
a motionless doll
his body on her body.

       You wanted it this way.
(This is the punishment for sluts
                           like you,
girls who let things happen.)

Doll

she sighs
when I take her out
the same dumb doll
who bleeds for me
she has one blue eye
the other is a hole
nothing is good about her
she is disfigured
her plastic limbs
scoured clean
with an iv line
she doesn't like me
she says terrible things
I feed her just the same
when she is done
I carry her back
to the bone yard where
the moon glitters
in her guise of white
her surface is darkness
I am not alone
a woman is here
she is blonde like me
strong as hell
miss world
misunderstood
her arm says let it bleed
together we scream
together we bury
that fucking doll
every single time

Stay

The lilies in the greenhouse—shiver,

                wither in dim light.

    It is raining.
    You drink your root beer,
    hope to keep it down.
    Put the guitar away.
    You're done with it.
    It's too late
    for a love letter,
    but you write one anyway.

    You load the shotgun,
    prepare the heroin one last time.
    Lay your wallet
    on the floor.
    Stab a pen through the note
    into a pot of soil.

In the morning fresh lilies will arrive—

                in the breath of first light.

Another Morning at the Starlight Hotel

Wet hair curls like brush strokes,
        around her bruised chin.

She slips into the black dress
        to leave him to wonder
        if she was real.

Pulse of morning, sun hits her eyes
        gulls mob the sidewalk
        over crumbs.

She heads south,
        in a delinquent body,
        still half-drunk on bottom shelf bourbon.

She leaves behind
        one last cigarette,
        perfectly ringed with red.

The Roses

Nights I walk, on shifting earth, winter vertigo,
        the bloodless roses, in the window, quiet.

Closer to dawn, mint tea in a china cup
        I understand them now, the roses,

Flushed pale pink. The tender envy of winter trees.

More Angel than Bird

A break—in relentless winter,

    A great blue heron
                               exposed
    in a creek bed.

His graceful neck
                twisted,

    wings spread, forever frozen in flight.

    The swallows,
                swifts, nighthawks

                          all followed the inner voice.
Why did he stay?

    For a moment I mourn him.

    Winter's cold raw hands—break me too.

Jasmine Fence

There is nothing but jasmine—
        down the length of the wood planked path,
           leafy with green anoles, that scatter in early sun.

Bees stab yellow pinwheel centers.

       I have fallen—away

             from myself—

Our belongings packed in moving boxes.

I ate the tart cherry Danish you bought at Sweet Caroline's.

I wear the morning kisses you gave me

        on cheeks, lips, eyelids,
        as delicate as the green tree frog that hides
        in the bright bromeliad.

Back home—where we started,
              breathing air,
                        thick with Florida jasmine.

Suicide, Sexy Bones, and Shoes That Just Might Fit

"Cinderella fit into the shoe like a love letter into its envelope."
                                        Anne Sexton

I planned to go to Dickinson's house
—how did I end up here? Forest Hills,
a cold fucking graveyard in Boston,
to court the sexy bones of Anne Sexton.

Was it because she did the impossible?
Sat at that damn typewriter,
trying to find the words—to live.
A housewife with a Pulitzer,
God in her typewriter
her pretty ones laid away in boxes—

I shiver where I sit, on the frost-bit
ground, gowned in new snow.
I pull my coat tighter,
and think about the day Anne died.
Lunch with Maxine, tuna sandwiches.
She hugged her friend goodbye
and said see you tomorrow.

Hours later she was found dead
in her garage. She wore
her mother's fur coat.
She was only forty-five.

I too have fought the good fight.
My big secret, twice I tried to die.
Strange. I love life
but sit with bones.

The Consolation of Flowers

I planted fresh roses in pots on the patio today
—a new ruby color
showered with the late
rain of a Florida summer storm.

Years have passed
        since I last tried to take my life.

The wintering is over.

I leave behind the roses,
        I leave behind the body,
           the river refused to keep.

The Great Dishonesty of the Precipice, Its Edge

Rock forward toward sheer drop
In your exhaustion, find the place beyond yourself, inside yourself,
note the height, the great peak, the valley below.

In your mind you see the same dark corner.
You know every inch of it.
Pace, forever pace, inside its walls.

Here on the rock's great face,
on its head you stand. Even the cliché of it cannot kill
this feeling, or the other who has no use for you,
the other who lives in the dark corner,
who even now wants you dead.
The voice tells you it will all stop,
the endless pacing, the dark corner.

You know what you needed to learn.
That the friable edge,
the great height above the abyss,
the cliff, the crag, it's not for fall,
but for flight, because even now the heart beats,
knows terror, knows that what lies at the bottom
of the pain's great weight is a circle of vultures.

A great weight you would not have others shoulder.
How cruel. And cruelty is not yours,
just love, love, love, love, love—
Love, that rescues us from ourselves,
even from death.

For at the great abyss,
we find not despair, but great wings
whose beating, even now fills
your ears with an endless whoosh
the plumping, plummeting
sound of it—wings
their beats dip and soar
above the sound of your indestructible heart.

ABOUT THE AUTHOR

Elizabeth Mercurio earned an MFA in poetry from The Solstice Low-Residency Program of Pine Manor College. Her work has appeared in *Third Point Press, Philadelphia Stories, The Skinny Poetry Journal, The Literary Nest, Fledgling Rag*, and *Lily Poetry Review*. She's a Best of the Net nominee and was the 2016 recipient of The Sharon Olds Fellowship for Poetry.

www.ingramcontent.com/pod-product-compliance
Lightning Source LLC
Chambersburg PA
CBHW071326080526
44587CB00018B/3355